THE NICHOLAS PARSONS QUIZ BOOK

The son of a doctor, Nicholas Parsons was born in Grantham, and educated at St Paul's School, London and Glasgow University. After completing an engineering apprenticeship on Clydebank, he appeared with local Repertory Companies in Glasgow and decided to become a full-time professional actor. He worked in Repertory at Bromley for three years, and then tried his hand at cabaret before launching out as a comedian at the Windmill Theatre, where he stayed six months. In 1952 he joined the BBC Drama Repertory Company. Here he also met Denise Bryer whom he later married: they now have two grown-up children. Nicholas has appeared in many television programmes, and was for ten years the straight man in the famous television partnership with the comedian, the late Arthur Haynes. In 1965 he returned to the theatre and starred for fifteen months in *Boeing Boeing*. In 1967 he received the Variety Club Award as Radio Personality of the Year for the satirical programme *Listen to this Space*. He has been chairman of radio's *Just a Minute* for thirteen years.

Perhaps he is most popularly known as the host and compere of Anglia Television's *Sale of the Century*, but he is in constant demand for other work both as an actor and solo artist. He has achieved a reputation as an after-dinner speaker, and has the distinction of being the joint holder of the longest after-dinner speech listed in the Guinness Book of Records: he spoke non-stop for eleven hours to help raise money for one of the children's charities in which he is involved.

THE NICHOLAS PARSONS QUIZ BOOK

A STAR BOOK
published by
the Paperback Division of
W. H. ALLEN & Co. Ltd

A Star Book
Published in 1980
by the Paperback Division of
W. H. Allen & Co. Ltd
A Howard and Wyndham Company
44 Hill Street, London W1X 8LB

Typeset by Computacomp (UK) Ltd
Fort William, Scotland
Printed in Great Britain by
Made and printed in Great Britain by
The Anchor Press Ltd, Tiptree, Essex
ISBN 0 352 30769 2

Nicholas Parsons wishes to thank Peter and David Lund for their help in the preparation of the questions, and Caxton Publications for their verification of the answers.

INTRODUCTION

Quiz games must surely be as old as the human race. Human beings have always played games, whether they be elaborate team games out of doors, or simple family entertainments in the home. During childhood, participation in knowledge games is an important part of growing up, and many adults continue to indulge in charades and guessing games at parties with even more enthusiasm than the children. This was particularly so before the era of television, and must have applied equally in ancient Rome and Greece. In Biblical times one could imagine programmes such as 'Double Your Shekels' or 'Brain of Judea', with the winner receiving a fatted calf, and the runner-up, a pint of fresh goat's milk.

The growth and popularity of television and increased airtime on radio during the last twenty years has raised the party game and quiz to a level of sophistication that must have previously seemed impossible. Such is the demand for new and entertaining ideas to fill all the hours of the week on television and radio that programme planners are increasingly attracted to the quiz format. With the escalating costs of production in all fields of entertainment, quiz programmes can be simple and economical to set up, while providing entertainment and interest together with the excitement and involvement that a media-educated public has grown to expect. The strong identification with the contestants which the viewer or listener is able to experience is the key to the success of these programmes. Critics complain, particularly of T.V. quizzes, that the large prizes on offer appeal to the viewers' avarice, but this is secondary to the excitement of the competition. One has only to think of the success of a programme like 'Mastermind' in which the contestants go through agonies, sitting alone on a raised chair under the glare of a spotlight and before a strange audience, while questions are fired at them in an inquisitorial manner against the clock ... and all for the honour of winning a glass bowl!

In the formal quiz the role of the Quiz Master has assumed a strange significance. While the spectator identifies with the contestants, he may, however, respond to the Chairman in a variety of ways. The Quiz Master plays the role of 'referee', or the voice of authority, and may inspire extreme responses depending on mood or temperament. Some may find him lenient, kind, helpful and considerate while to others his performance may appear overbearing, abrupt, pompous or unreasonable: he is the popular 'fall-guy'. The letters received by Quiz Masters of television and radio panel shows bear this out. Some letters complain of bias towards one of the contestants while others, referring to the same incident, completely contradict the allegation. So really, the Chairman is the only contributor to the programme who simply cannot win!

The popularity of quizzes, which has been exploited by the media in all its forms, including the newspapers, has resulted in what can only be described as a 'quiz-conscious society'. I have heard people in conversation say, 'I would like to ask you a question', and the other person replies, 'How much do I get for the right answer?'

If people are exposed to all this information they must feel a need to show off their knowledge, and a desire to share the many facts that they have acquired, thus producing a happy atmosphere and a healthy sense of competition. Imagine the situation on the London Underground—a tube train, packed with commuters, comes to a halt; there is a hold up. But does the talk turn to the usual conversational gambits of the British: the weather, the test match or the Government? No, these days the conversation of strangers is much more illuminating and exciting: 'Do you know how many breakdowns there are every year on the London Underground?' 'Did you know the London Underground is the longest railway system in the world?' 'Do you know why the Underground is called the tube?' 'Can you tell me how many stations there are between here and Cockfosters?' 'Which is the deepest underground railway station?' 'Which station has the most moving staircases?' 'Who designed the London Underground?' 'When was the Jubilee Line opened?' ... And so the conversation flows back and forth, question after question, with answers following quick and fast. A real sense of camaraderie is built up, as the discomfort and frustration of the breakdown is forgotten in the happy atmosphere of the shared knowledge.

If this atmosphere does not already exist, it must surely be only a matter of time before it does; and if this book can contribute anything towards that delightful situation, and at the same time give pleasure to all the family, then the effort of preparing the questions will have been more than worth the time involved.

In a quiz book it is possible to present elaborate questions to the reader which would not be appropriate in other types of media. There is time to study individual questions at length, and consequently the reader may arrive at a considered answer in a way which would not be possible in a public contest. My friends Peter and David Lund and I have researched a large number of unusual and intrinsically interesting facts on which we have based the questions in this book. In the GENERAL SECTION, all the questions require a single answer and cover a good standard of general knowledge. The reader is invited to attempt all the subjects to see in which areas he performs best. The SPECIALIST SECTION includes a variety of forms of questions, and requires a more detailed knowledge so the reader would tend to score well only in his specialist subjects. In the FUN SECTION the questions are intended primarily to amuse. The facts presented are designed to be entertaining in themselves and may be rather obscure. A greater element of luck is therefore present, and consequently the reader may like to award himself bonus marks for ingenious wrong answers.

The method of scoring is extremely simple. A maximum of 20 marks can be obtained for each subject with one mark for each question or part question, as indicated. The answers for each subject (dare I call this the 'Parsons Knows'?) are on the back of the page which lists the questions. This should appeal particularly to the cheats! The reader may rate his performance as follows:

15–20 marks	You must have cheated!
10–14 marks	Are you sure you didn't cheat?
Below 10 marks	Perhaps you should have cheated!

I hope that the questions in the book prove to be both interesting and informative. Above all, we have made every effort to be entertaining. May I wish all readers the best of luck!

NICHOLAS PARSONS
June 1980

GENERAL SECTION

MOVIE MATINEE	(Films)
IT'S ON THE BOX	(Television)
BE A SPORT	(Sport—General)
HOBBIES CORNER	(Hobbies and Pastimes)
THE BEST OF BRITISH	(Geography of the UK)
WHAT'S COOKING?	(Cooking and Eating Out)
MAKE IT A DATE	(British History)
PULL UP A PEW WITH PARSONS	(Bible and Religion)
READERS DIGEST THIS	(Popular Books and Novels)
FOR TOP OF THE POPSTERS	(Popular Music)

MOVIE MATINEE

1. Name the actor who played the part of Count Dracula in the original Hollywood film made in 1931.

2. Who were Wolf J. Flywheel, J. Cleever Loophole and S. Quentin Quale?

3. Name the film made in 1967 in which David Niven played the part of James Bond.

4. Name the British actress who played the part of an American in her two most famous screen roles: Scarlett O'Hara and Blanche Dubois.

5. Name the comedy duo who had screen encounters with Frankenstein, Dr Jekyll and Mr Hyde, the Invisible Man and the Mummy.

6. Who took the part of the young boy who idolised his drunken, rundown boxer father in the original 1931 version of *The Champ*?

7. What was the name of the Billy Wilder comedy in which Jack Lemmon and Tony Curtis take the part of two jazz musicians and appear in drag?

8. Who played the part of the prospective bridegroom in the film *Guess Who's Coming to Dinner*?

9. What was the name of the famous actress whose first starring role in a talking picture was Anna Christie, in the film of the same name made in 1930?

10. Who played the part of the younger Brando in *The Godfather Part 2*?

11. Who was the French comedian who created the character of Monsieur Hulot?

MOVIE MATINEE—ANSWERS

1. Bela Lugosi.

2. They were all characters played by Groucho Marx in the Marx Brothers' films.

3. *Casino Royale*.

4. Vivien Leigh.

5. Abbott and Costello.

6. Jackie Cooper.

7. *Some Like it Hot*.

8. Sidney Poitier.

9. Greta Garbo.

10. Robert de Niro.

11. Jacques Tati.

12. Which British Director, whose distinguished career spanned over 50 years, made his first feature film in 1925, *The Pleasure Garden*?

13. What is the name of the Swedish film director who achieved great critical acclaim with his film, *The Seventh Seal*, made in 1957, in which a knight, returning from the Crusades, challenges Death to a game of chess by the sea shore?

14. Who was the Blonde preferred by Gentlemen in the musical version of the twenties satire, released in 1953?

15. Name the child actor who played the title role in David Lean's cinematic version of *Oliver Twist* and later became the television director of *Monty Python's Flying Circus*.

16. What was the name of the Biblical epic in 1953, which was the first film to be made in Cinemascope?

17. What was the name of Francois Truffaut's 1973 Oscar winning film which was all about the making of a film?

18. Peter Finch starred in the much acclaimed film *The Trials of Oscar Wilde*. Another film on the same subject was shot simultaneously, and called *Oscar Wilde*. Who starred as Wilde in that film?

19. What is the name of the outstanding German film in which Marlene Dietrich, playing the part of a tawdry night-club singer, sang *Falling in Love Again*, a song with which she is still associated to this day?

20. Name the famous Ealing comedy in which an impecunious heir eliminates eight distinguished members of the D'Ascoyne family, all played by Alec Guinness, who stand between him and the family fortune.

12. Alfred Hitchcock.

13. Ingmar Bergman.

14. Marilyn Monroe.

15. John Howard Davies.

16. *The Robe*.

17. *Day For Night*.

18. Robert Morley.

19. *The Blue Angel*, 1930.

20. *Kind Hearts and Coronets*, 1940.

IT'S ON THE BOX

1. In which year was the world's first public television service introduced at Alexandra Palace?

2. Which is the longest-running television serial in this country?

3. Name the television programme which regularly helps New Scotland Yard in its fight against crime.

4. Name the popular BBC series which was set in a mining community in the North East of England after the First World War.

5. In which television programme have Robin Day, Dave Allen, Ken Dodd, Denis Healey and Eddie Waring regularly featured?

6. Which was the first panel game series to be shown on British television?

7. Name the comedian who played an American army sergeant with a compulsion for gambling, in a long-running television series.

8. What do Captain Kremmen, Sid Snot and 'Angry of Mayfair' have in common?

9. What was the name of the school which was featured in the ITV *Please Sir* series?

10. What was the name of the first of the celebrated late night television satire shows which was usually referred to by its initials?

IT'S ON THE BOX—ANSWERS

1. 1936.
2. *Coronation Street.*
3. *Police Five*—introduced by Shaw Taylor.
4. *When the Boat Comes In.*
5. *Mike Yarwood in Persons.*
6. *What's My Line?*
7. Phil Silvers (Sgt. Bilko).
8. All are featured in the *Kenny Everett Video Show.*
9. Fenn Street School.
10. *That Was The Week That Was.*

11. Which popular television series has starred in succession Honor Blackman, Diana Rigg, Linda Thorsen?

12. Who is responsible on television for *Potty Time*?

13. Who was the first person to use the most taboo four letter expletive on British television?

14. What is the popular programme that has the alternative title of *Jeux Sans Frontières*?

15. Who was the well-known broadcaster who began as a war correspondent and for many years introduced *Panorama* every week? (There is now a lecture delivered in his honour every year).

16. When ITV first started, what was the title of the long-running weekend variety programme which was originally compered by Tommy Trinder, and then by Bruce Forsythe?

17. What is the name of the Captain played by Arthur Lowe in the popular television series *Dad's Army*?

18. Who was the real life person on whom the successful television serial *Jennie*, starring Lee Remick, was based?

19. What was the title of the documentary programme, first shown in 1979, which received a great deal of publicity because it dealt with the difficult social problem of young teenagers who leave home and arrive in London without any money, friends or even contacts?

20. Who was the British comedian who had a very popular television series in the sixties, in which he played among other things a loveable tramp? (The actor who played his straight man is still seen regularly on television today).

IT'S ON THE BOX—ANSWERS

11. *The Avengers.*

12. Michael Bentine.

13. Kenneth Tynan.

14. *It's A Knockout.*

15. Richard Dimbleby.

16. *Sunday Night At The London Palladium.*

17. Captain Mainwaring.

18. Lady Randolph Churchill.

19. *Johnny Go Home.*

20. Arthur Haynes.
    Note: You can gain a bonus point if you know the name of his straight man. The answer to this is on the cover of the book.

BE A SPORT

1. Which football team plays its home matches at the baseball ground?
2. Name the member of the aristocracy who, in 1867, introduced the rules of boxing, which still bear his name.
3. Near which town is the classic horse race, the St Leger, run?
4. When Bjorn Borg won the men's singles at Wimbledon for the fourth successive year, whose record did he beat?
5. The Eisenhower trophy is the world amateur team championship for which major sport?
6. Where in France does the famous 24-hour motor race take place?
7. At which bridge does the Oxford and Cambridge Boat Race begin?
8. In which London stadium is the Greyhound Derby held each year?
9. What is the name of the contest played between the winners of the National and American leagues as a climax to the USA baseball season?
10. In which country did the game of snooker originate?

BE A SPORT—ANSWERS

1. Derby County.
2. The Marquess of Queensberry.
3. Doncaster.
4. Fred Perry. (Wimbledon Men's singles holder 1934, '35, '36).
5. Golf.
6. Le Mans.
7. Putney Bridge.
8. White City.
9. The World Series.
10. Snooker originated in India in 1875.

BE A SPORT

11. At which sport has Britain produced world champions David Wilkie and Duncan Goodhew?

12. A game of football begins with a kick-off. What is the term or expression used to begin a game of hockey?

13. With which sport is the Isle of Man particularly associated?

14. In the game of squash how many points do you require to win a game, providing you are two points clear of your opponent?

15. With which sport in Britain do you associate the Milk Race?

16. Tigre, Flanagan and Psalm are well-known names associated with which activity?

17. With which sport do you associate the Tampa Bay Rowdies?

18. How does a team qualify for the Rugby Union Triple Crown?

19. In which sport are there two different kinds of court, one known as the Eton version, and the other the Rugby version?

20. In which sport can you refer to the participants as 'Toxophilites'?

BE A SPORT—ANSWERS

11. Swimming.

12. A bully-off.

13. Motor-cycle racing.

14. 9 (at 8 all, the players continue until one has a lead of 2).

15. Cycling.

16. Show Jumping (they are the names of horses, all show-jumping champions).

17. Football (it is an American soccer team).

18. The Triple Crown is won when any one of the four home counties defeats all the others in one season.

19. Fives.

20. Archery.

HOBBIES CORNER

1. What hobby or pastime would you enjoy if you were doing 'dressage'?

2. If you were a coin collector and owned a 'bun' penny, what would you have in your collection?

3. If you heard someone speaking about F-stops, filters and ASA's, with which hobby would he be associated?

4. How many tricks would be taken in a bridge contract to achieve a small slam?

5. If you were a 'do-it-yourself' enthusiast, where in your house would you normally fit architrave?

6. In which pastime would you use a spinnaker?

7. If someone possessed an Ena Harkness, an Albertine, and a General MacArthur, what would you assume was their hobby?

8. How many pieces would each player have on the board at the beginning of a game of chess?

9. If you were engaged in petit point, what would you be doing?

10. If you collected antiques, to what part of a piece of furniture would you be referring if you talked about 'cabriole'?

HOBBIES CORNER—ANSWERS

1. Horse riding.

2. An early Queen Victoria penny with the 'young' head.

3. Photography.

4. 12 tricks.

5. Around a door or window. It is specially shaped timber which you buy for this purpose.

6. Sailing.

7. Gardening: they are all names of rose trees.

8. 16.

9. Needlework or tapestry.

10. Legs.

11. If you had in your collection a Painted Lady, a Camberwell Beauty and a Peacock, what would your hobby be?

12. If you heard someone talking about maturation, fining, must and lees, in what would you assume they were interested?

13. Which seasonal activity begins on the 'Glorious Twelfth'?

14. If you were doing Ikebana, what would your hobby be?

15. What is the pastime, still popular today and said to date back in England to the time of Edward I, in which the participants wear special costumes, and sometimes employ a hobby-horse?

16. With which activity or pastime would you associate a Spelaeologist?

17. What would be the hobby of someone who could create something by interpreting the instructions given by the following abbreviations: Tw.2k., C.4F., B.1., M.B.4., Cr.3F., Mv.2, P.Sl.s., K.s.s.b., Cr.2 B.P.?

18. If someone said they were tinkering with their De Dion Bouton or their Delarge, what would you assume was their hobby?

19. What would be the hobby of someone interested in Bulbuls, Shrikes, Motmots, Rollers, Colies, Todies, Potoos or Auks?

20. The world's most valuable postage stamp was sold in New York for 850,000 dollars on the 5th April 1980. From which former British Colony did the stamp originate?

11. Collecting butterflies.

12. Wine making.

13. Grouse shooting.

14. Flower arrangement. It's the Japanese art of flower arrangement.

15. Morris dancing.

16. Exploring caves and pot-holes.

17. Knitting.

18. Vintage motor cars.

19. Ornithology (or bird watching). They are all species of birds found in the different countries of the world.

20. British Guiana (now Guyana) 1856 one cent stamp. This stamp is the only specimen of a specially printed batch still in existence.

THE BEST OF BRITISH

1. Which city lies almost exactly half way between London and John O'Groats?

2. Which is *now* the smallest county in the British Isles?

3. Which river divides Stockton from Middlesborough?

4. Where do Watkin's Path, Llanberis Way, the Pigtrack and the Horseshoe lead to?

5. For which festival is Nottingham traditionally famous?

6. Whereabouts in England would you find Wales?

7. Before the new county areas were created, Yorkshire was divided into three separate areas: North, West and East. What was the name given to these three areas?

8. Name the small island off the Cornish coast which is thought to be part of the lost kingdom of Lyonesse.

9. Which is the nearer to London by road: Edinburgh or Glasgow?

10. What is the name of the famous Spa town in the Peak District which is said to compete with the glories of Bath?

THE BEST OF BRITISH—ANSWERS

1. Newcastle-upon-Tyne.
2. The Isle of Wight.
3. The River Tees.
4. The top of Snowdon.
5. The Goose Fair.
6. Wales is a village in Yorkshire, south-east of Rotherham.
7. Ridings.
8. St Michael's Mount.
9. Edinburgh: 372 miles. (Glasgow 389 miles).
10. Buxton.

11. What is the name of the well-known landmark and beauty spot near the town of Eastbourne?

12. What is the name of the hills which are on the border of England and Scotland?

13. In which county of England is the Royal Residence of Sandringham?

14. In which area of the British Isles would you find St Mary's, St Agnes and Bryher?

15. In what part of the British Isles is there a picturesque area, much enjoyed by tourists, called the Giant's Causeway?

16. Which is the largest natural lake in England?

17. Which of the Channel Islands is nearest to the French Coast?

18. Which city in Pembrokeshire is the smallest cathedral city in Great Britain?

19. What is the area in the Highlands of Scotland which has been developed as a popular sporting centre, particularly for skiing?

20. In which county in England would you find the Dukeries?

11. Beachy Head.

12. Cheviots.

13. Norfolk.

14. The Scilly Isles.

15. On the coast of County Antrim, Northern Ireland.

16. Lake Windermere, in the Lake District.

17. Alderney.

18. St David's.

19. The Cairngorms.

20. Nottinghamshire.

WHAT'S COOKING?

1. At what meal would you expect to enjoy a Maid of Honour?

2. Which country features Sukiyaki as its most famous national dish?

3. What is the difference between an 'A la Carte' and a 'Table D'hôte' menu?

4. What are Pomfret Cakes?

5. Name the dish created by Master Chef Escoffier, at the Savoy Hotel, in honour of a famous opera singer.

6. What is a roux used for in cooking?

7. What is the main vegetable used in the preparation of the Russian soup Borsch (or bortsch)?

8. What animal was traditionally used to assist in the gathering of the edible fungi, truffles?

9. What is the major ingredient of a Sauce Lyonnaise?

10. Which part of a sheep is used to hold the ingredients contained in a Haggis?

WHAT'S COOKING?—ANSWERS

1. Tea. It is a small individual tart of light puff pastry, with a filling made of egg, ground almonds and lemon. History relates that Anne Boleyn, then a maid of honour at the English court, first made these cakes in the hope of pleasing Henry VIII, who, finding them delicious, named them after their creator.

2. Japan.

3. 'Table D'hôte' is a set menu at a set price, and 'A la Carte' is an individual choice of dishes.

4. Sweets made from liquorice, more commonly known as Pontefract cakes.

5. Peach Melba (named after Dame Nellie Melba).

6. To thicken sauce.

7. Beetroot.

8. Pigs (More commonly nowadays specially trained dogs, which locate the fungus).

9. Onions.

10. Stomach.

11. What is the vegetable, of which there are two quite different varieties, Globe and Jerusalem?

12. Besides sugar and egg-white, what is the other principal ingredient of the Italian dish Zabaglione which gives it the characteristic flavour?

13. From what is Pâté de Foie Gras traditionally made?

14. Crottin de Chavignol, Roquefort en Tranches and Petit Munster are all varieties of what type of food?

15. What species of fish is used to produce bloaters?

16. If you ordered an oyster in a butcher's shop what kind of meat would he serve to you?

17. Which food do we obtain from the roots of the Cassava plant?

18. What type of fruit is included in the traditional fermentation process used to produce Sauerkraut?

19. On what national menu would you be likely to see Voolab Jamon, Jellabies, Tho-Thole, Pootoo Rice Balls and Soojee Poorees?

20. What would a diner be eating if he had been served with a portion of lamb's fries?

11. Artichoke.

12. Marsala wine.

13. Goose livers.

14. All are cheeses.

15. Bloaters are lightly smoked herrings.

16. Veal. The oyster is the shoulder of veal from which the fore knuckle has been removed.

17. Tapioca.

18. Juniper berries.

19. Indian.

20. The testicles of the male animal, which are considered a great delicacy. Fries are usually obtained from lambs 2–3 months old.

MAKE IT A DATE

1. The ancient Britons were of which race?

2. Did Julius Caesar invade England before or after the birth of Christ?

3. Which great Saxon king ordered the building of Westminister Abbey?

4. Name the Norman king who came to the throne after the death of William the Conqueror and was killed by an arrow while hunting in the New Forest.

5. Which King of England spent no more than six months of his 10-year reign in his native country?

6. Who was the leader of the Peasant's Revolt against the unjust laws and grinding taxes imposed by Richard II?

7. What fate was inflicted on Queen Isabella, who had been responsible for the imprisonment (and possibly the murder) of her husband Edward II, when Edward III came to the throne?

8. Where did the famous battle take place in 1415 in which Henry V defeated the French?

9. What was the name of the battle which brought the Wars of the Roses to an end, and Henry Tudor to the throne of England?

10. Which of Henry VIII's six wives kept her head and survived him, by just one year, after his death in 1547?

MAKE IT A DATE—ANSWERS

1. The Celtic race.
2. Before Christ: 55 BC.
3. Edward the Confessor (1042–66).
4. William Rufus (William II).
5. Richard I.
6. Wat Tyler.
7. She was sent to a nunnery.
8. Agincourt.
9. The Battle of Bosworth Field.
10. Catherine Parr (died 1548).

11. What was the name of the Evangelist Preacher, who followed the teachings of Calvin, and was principally responsible for bringing the Protestant Faith to Scotland?

12. How were Elizabeth I and Mary Queen of Scots related?

13. Of which famous act of treachery were Thomas Winter and Robert Catesby the main instigators? (A fellow conspirator is the person who is best remembered for this treason today).

14. Which King enjoyed being known as the 'merry monarch' because of his enslavement to 'a fantastical gentleman called Cupid'?

15. Who was the last Stuart King to rule Britain?

16. Which King of England could not speak any English and communicated with his ministers throughout his reign in French and Latin?

17. Which famous incident, off the East coast of America, is considered to be principally responsible for precipitating the American War of Independence whereby Britain lost her American Colonies?

18. Which King ruled England for the whole of the Napoleonic wars and has gone down in history as 'the mad King'?

19. Which King was the founder and first monarch of the House of Windsor?

20. How many years was Queen Victoria on the throne?

MAKE IT A DATE—ANSWERS

11. John Knox.

12. They were cousins.

13. The Gunpowder Plot. Guy Fawkes was only a subordinate brought in by Winter.

14. Charles II.

15. James II (Queen Anne was the last of the Stuart Monarchs).

16. George I.

17. The Boston Tea Party.

18. George III.

19. George V.

20. 64 years.

PULL UP A PEW WITH PARSONS

1. Which of the Gospels is generally regarded to have been written first?

2. How old was Jesus at the time of His crucifixion?

3. Who is considered to be the author of the Acts of the Apostles?

4. Was St Paul one of the 12 original apostles?

5. Which prayer did Jesus teach to His disciples during the Sermon on the Mount?

6. Which of the virtues Faith, Hope and Charity are Christians taught to be the greatest of the three?

7. In which Book of the Old Testament are the Ten Commandments first listed?

8. Which is the sixth Commandment?

9. Where in the Bible would you find the story of Samson and Delilah?

10. To whom is the 23rd Psalm attributed?

11. How were David and Solomon related?

12. Which is the largest Cathedral in the world?

PULL UP A PEW WITH PARSONS—ANSWERS

1. The Gospel according to St Mark.
2. 33.
3. St Luke.
4. No.
5. The Lord's Prayer (Our Father).
6. Charity.
7. Exodus.
8. Thou shalt not kill.
9. The Book of Judges.
10. The Psalm of David.
11. Father and son.
12. St John the Divine, the Cathedral Church of the Diocese of New York. It can accommodate 10,000 worshippers at any one time.

13. What is the name of the small Norman Church in West Smithfield, which is the only Church in the city of London not to be destroyed in the great fire of 1666?

14. At which Church of England Service would you expect to hear the 'Magnificat' and the 'Nunc Dimittis'?

15. Who founded the Protestant movement?

16. What is the name of the administrative centre of the Roman Catholic Church?

17. What is the Apocrypha?

18. Which 17th-century King commanded 54 scholars to write a new translation of the Bible using the language of the people? This particular Bible is often still referred to, using the King's name.

19. What was the name of the book, first published in 1963, written by the then Bishop of Woolwich, Dr John Robinson, which challenged many of the fundamental beliefs in the Christian Faith?

20. A choirboy wears his cassock but what does he do with his hassock?

13. St Bartholomew-the-Great. (Next to Bart's Hospital).

14. Evensong.

15. Martin Luther.

16. The Vatican.

17. Old Testament books, not counted genuine by the Jews, and excluded from the Canon at the Reformation.

18. James I.

19. *Honest to God*.

20. He would kneel on it.
    A cassock is the garment worn by a chorister under his white surplice.
    A hassock is the kneeling cushion used in Church.

READERS DIGEST THIS

1. What is the name of the lady detective who appears in some of the novels by Agatha Christie?

2. Who was the author of the exciting Hornblower adventures?

3. Name the popular American writer who took to a life of activities such as big-game hunting and deep-sea fishing, and also enjoyed the spectacle of bull-fighting.

4. What was the name of the central character in Joyce's novel *A Portrait of the Artist as a Young Man*?

5. Who wrote the novel which tells the story of the relationship between a gamekeeper and the wife of a crippled intellectual? (This book also became the subject of a famous court case.)

6. Name the popular writer who has written several novels including *The Guns of Navarone* and *Where Eagles Dare* which have been made into successful films.

7. In which book is Mowgli the principal character?

8. Name the Russian author who was awarded a Nobel Prize and wrote *Doctor Zhivago*.

9. Who was the Secretary to the Admiralty in the late seventeenth century who wrote about the Fire of London and other happenings of his day?

10. What was the name of the island in which Gulliver discovered a race of little people in Swift's *Gulliver's Travels*?

11. Which of Graham Greene's well known novels is referred to as the tale of the 'Whisky Priest'?

READERS DIGEST THIS—ANSWERS

1. Miss Marple.
2. C. S. Forester.
3. Ernest Hemingway.
4. Stephen Daedalus. (Stephen D).
5. D. H. Lawrence (the novel was *Lady Chatterley's Lover*).
6. Alistair Maclean.
7. *The Jungle Book* by Rudyard Kipling.
8. Boris Pasternak.
9. Samuel Pepys (1633–1703).
10. Lilliput.
11. *The Power and the Glory*.

12. In which of Dickens's novels does Mr Wackford Squeers, the Yorkshire schoolmaster, appear?

13. Name the popular Victorian novelist who created such characters as Mr Sponge, Mr Pig, Mr Swell and Mr Jorrocks in his stories concerning the English hunting fraternity.

14. In which street in London's West End was the celebrated detective, created by Sir Arthur Conan Doyle, supposed to reside?

15. Name the writer who has written a book about Jack the ripper, but is better known for his light-hearted novels concerning the medical profession.

16. Name the central character, in the novels of P. G. Wodehouse, who is saved from total disaster only by the resources of his butler, the inimitable Jeeves.

17. What is the name of the successful novel by Frederick Forsyth about a plot to assassinate General Charles de Gaulle?

18. Who wrote two bestselling books concerning her attempts to raise Elsa the lioness?

19. What was the name of Frederic Raphael's novel which led to a highly successful television series which explored the changing attitudes and styles of a generation that went to Cambridge in the fifties?

20. What is the name of the bestselling novelist who wrote a number of historical novels and adventure stories but is perhaps best remembered for his exploration of the Black Magic cult in such books as *The Devil Rides Out*?

12. *Nicholas Nickleby.*

13. R. S. Surtees.

14. Sherlock Holmes had his rooms in Baker Street.

15. Richard Gordon.

16. Bertie Wooster.

17. *The Day of the Jackal.*

18. Joy Adamson.

19. *The Glittering Prizes.*

20. Dennis Wheatley.

TOP OF THE POPSTERS

1. Which was the bestselling 78 record of all time?

2. Which of the famous four, John, Paul, Ringo and George, was not an original founder member of the Beatles?

3. What was the name of the song from *Evita* which became a hit record before the show was produced?

4. Which group reached the top of the charts in April 1980 by *Going Underground*?

5. Name the well known pop singer whose real name was Mark Feld.

6. Which American pop singer of the early fifties was able to cry—probably all the way to the bank—as a result of both sides of his hit single?

7. From which Gershwin musical come the well-known songs *Summertime* and *I Got Plenty of Nuthin'*?

8. Which group released a bestselling album *Duke* at Easter 1980 which had no connection with the music of Duke Ellington?

9. Which Popular music composer was responsible for the evergreens *Easy to Love*, *I Love You*, and *At Long Last Love*?

10. Which record featuring Paul McCartney has sold the most copies?

11. Name the jazz musician who had a very big hit record with his own composition titled *Take Five*.

TOP OF THE POPSTERS—ANSWERS

1. *White Christmas* by Bing Crosby. It has been frequently re-issued and still sells today.

2. Ringo Starr.

3. *Don't Cry For Me, Argentina*.

4. The Jam.

5. Marc Bolan.

6. Johnnie Ray. *Cry* and *The Little White Cloud that Cried*.

7. *Porgy And Bess*.

8. Genesis.

9. Cole Porter.

10. *Mull of Kintyre* by Wings.

11. Dave Brubeck.

12. What was the title of Elvis Presley's first major hit record?

13. In the first ever chart, published in the *New Musical Express* on 14th November 1952, the top song was called *Here In My Heart*. Who was the singer of this hit recording? (He made a guest appearance in the film *The Godfather*).

14. What was the name of the hit record in 1961, featuring the clarinet of Acker Bilk, which remained in the charts for 55 weeks?

15. What was the name of the first Elton John record to reach the charts?

16. What was the name of the very familiar song, recorded by a German children's choir in 1954, which became an unlikely hit and is now a part of the community song repertoire in the English version?

17. What was the name of the Irish girl singer who had a number of hit records in the fifties including *Softly, Softly*, *Heartbeat*, and *Evermore*?

18. What was the name of the old Glenn Miller number which first brought Manhattan Transfer into the British charts?

19. Tony Bennett 'left his heart in San Francisco', but who reached number 1 in the charts in 1967 with another hit called *San Francisco (Be Sure to Wear Flowers in Your Hair)*?

20. With which group did Alan Price first achieve fame in the pop scene of the sixties?

TOP OF THE POPSTERS—ANSWERS

12. *Heartbreak Hotel.*

13. Al Martino.

14. *Stranger on the Shore.*

15. *Your Song.*

16. *Happy Wanderer* by the Obernkirchen Children's Choir.

17. Ruby Murray.

18. *Tuxedo Junction* 7th February 1976.

19. Scott McKenzie.

20. The Animals.

SPECIALIST SECTION

THE SHOW MUST GO ON	(Theatre)
HIT FOR SIX	(Cricket)
NATURE LOVERS STOP HERE	(Natural History)
FOR THOSE WITH AN EAR FOR MUSIC	(Classical Music and Jazz)
BOOKWORMS BROWSE HERE	(Literature and Poetry)
FOOD FOR THOUGHT	(Nutrition and Diet)
VINTAGE STUFF FOR WINE BUFFS	(Wines and Spirits)
TRAVEL BROADENS THE MIND	(World Geography)
FOR THE CULTURE VULTURE	(Art and Sculpture)
THE SCIENTIFIC WAY	(Science)

THE SHOW MUST GO ON

1. Which is the oldest existing theatre in England still used for regular public performances?

2. *The Mousetrap* is London's longest-running show, but which production is still running in New York after more than twenty years?

3. Name the distinguished knight of the theatre who appeared as Katherine in *The Taming of the Shrew* at the Stratford Memorial Theatre when he was a 14-year-old schoolboy.

4. What is the name of Alec McCowen's most unusual one man show?

5. In which play, written by Samuel Beckett, is the central character buried up to her waist in the first half and up to her neck after the interval?

6. What are the names of the open stage, proscenium stage and small auditorium which together make up the National Theatre complex in London?

   (3 MARKS)

7. What are the place names which go to complete the following Elizabethan and Jacobean plays?

   a. *The Duchess of* ____________
   b. *The Jew of* ____________
   c. *Two Gentlemen of* ____________
   d. *The Witch of* ____________

   (4 MARKS)

THE SHOW MUST GO ON—ANSWERS

1. Theatre Royal, Bristol. (Bristol Old Vic Company).

2. *The Fantasticks* running at the Playhouse, Greenwich Village.

3. Sir Laurence Olivier.

4. *The Gospel According to Saint Mark.*

5. *Happy Days.*

6. The Olivier Theatre, Lyttelton Theatre and Cottesloe Theatre.

7. a. *The Duchess of Malfi.*
   b. *The Jew of Malta.*
   c. *Two Gentlemen of Verona.*
   d. *The Witch of Edmonton.*

8. In which play by Henrik Ibsen, which shares the same title as a suite of music composed by Edvard Greig, are there characters named Trolls and a Button Moulder?

9. Which successful dramatist wrote three popular plays in the thirties, all of which had a theme concerned with time theories, one of which was called *Time and the Conways*, in which the three acts appear not to be in chronological order?

10. What is the play by Noel Coward, which has been revived many times, in which the two leading characters are called Elyot and Amanda?

11. What is the name of the modern dramatist, originally associated with the Royal Court Theatre in London, well-known for a trilogy of plays involving the same central characters and their political ideals?

12. Brush up your Shakespeare!
    a. *The Merry Wives of Windsor* tells of the amorous exploits of Sir John Falstaff. What was the name of the first play written by Shakespeare in which the character of Falstaff appears?
    b. Which of Shakespeare's comedies do most experts consider to be the first to have been written?

(2 MARKS)

13. Be sure of your Shaw!
    a. In which of Shaw's plays is the central character a member of the Salvation Army?
    b. In which of Shaw's plays is there a nurse who is called Ftatateeta?

(2 MARKS)

8. *Peer Gynt.*

9. J. B. Priestley. The other plays were *Dangerous Corner* and *I Have Been Here Before.*

10. *Private Lives.*

11. Arnold Wesker. The plays were *Chicken Soup With Barley*, *Roots*, and *I'm Talking About Jerusalem.*

12. a. *Henry IV Part I.* Falstaff also appears in *Henry IV Part II* and there are references to him in other plays.
    b. *The Comedy of Errors*, 1592–93.

13. a. *Major Barbara.*
    b. *Caesar and Cleopatra.*

HIT FOR SIX

1. What is the name of the Hampshire village which gave its name to the first cricket club to be formed in England, with its ground sited on Broad Halfpenny and Windmill Downs?

2. For what do the initials M.C.C. stand?

3. The highest number of wickets taken by one bowler in a single cricket match was 19, at the Manchester Test Match against the Australians in 1956. Who was the bowler?

4. Who was the first West Indian cricketer to be knighted? (He also played in Lancashire League Cricket).

5. In what respect are cricketers Chris Old of Yorkshire and Phil Edmonds of Middlesex exact opposites with the bat and ball?

6. Name the bowler who invented the googly. His son was a well-known television newsreader.

7. Who is the South African cricketer who has played many seasons for Worcestershire, became a naturalised British Subject, and has played for England?

8. Which county side did the following legendary cricketers represent during their first class cricketing careers?
   a. W. G. Grace b. F. E. Woolley c. J. B. Hobbs
   (3 MARKS)

9. Under the present rules of cricket, in a three day County Match, to how many overs is the opening side restricted?

10. What unique record was achieved by Garfield Sobers in a county championship match between Nottinghamshire and Glamorgan in 1968?

HIT FOR SIX—ANSWERS

1. Hambledon.

2. Marylebone Cricket Club.

3. Jim Laker.

4. Sir Learie Constantine.

5. Chris Old is a fast right arm bowler who bats left-handed. Phil Edmonds is a slow left arm bowler who bats right-handed.

6. B. J. T. Bosanquet.

7. Basil D'Olivera.

8. a. Gloucestershire. b. Kent. c. Surrey.

9. 100.

10. He hit six sixes in one over.

11. *Cricket Captains:*
    a. Who was the Captain of the England team in Australia during the controversial Bodyline series before the war?
    b. Who was the Captain of the Australian team against whom Hutton scored his record 364 in the timeless test at the Oval in 1938? (This player had previously held the highest individual test match record score in tests between England and Australia).
    c. Who was the professional cricketer who became an amateur in order to be eligible to captain England, which he subsequently did?

(3 MARKS)

12. Who was the famous Middlesex and England cricketer who played in 78 Tests and also played football for Arsenal?

13. Geoff Boycott, one of the most prolific of run scorers, had the distinction of becoming only the third Yorkshire batsmen to hit 100 centuries in first class cricket.
    Name the previous two Yorkshiremen to pass this landmark.

(2 MARKS)

14. In the 1979 cricket season there were two unique doubles, with the four major trophies being won by two counties.
    Which county captured:
    a. The Gillette Cup
       The John Player League
    b. The Benson and Hedges Cup
       The Schweppes County Championship?

(2 MARKS)

11. a. Douglas Jardine.
    b. Don Bradman.
    c. W. R. Hammond.

12. Denis Compton.

13. H. Sutcliffe (149 centuries).
    L. Hutton (129 centuries).

14. a. Somerset.
    b. Essex.

NATURE LOVERS STOP HERE

1. What is the main difference between a male and female snail?

2. Are some plants able to feel pain?

3. How many legs has a Daddy Longlegs?

4. How many bones are there in the human body? (Approximately)

5. In the botanical sense, which of the following is correctly described as a fruit: mushroom, tomato or rhubarb?

6. Which creature, not extinct, is:
   a. The fastest swimming bird?
   b. The largest member of the deer family?
   c. The largest mammal?

   (3 MARKS)

7. What is the collective name for a group of the following animals?
   a. Lions.
   b. Squirrels.

   (2 MARKS)

8. What is the collective name for a group of the following birds?
   a. Geese.
   b. Partridges.

   (2 MARKS)

NATURE LOVERS STOP HERE—ANSWERS

1. No difference. The snail is an hermaphrodite.

2. Probably not. Plants do not have a central nervous system, although some scientists have claimed to have performed experiments which somehow 'demonstrate' pain.

3. All spiders have 8 legs. The harvestman or 'Daddy Longlegs' is a member of the spider family.

4. Approximately 200.

5. The tomato is a fruit, the mushroom a fungus, but rhubarb, though described as fruit on a menu, in the botanical sense is not a fruit.

6. a. The penguin, (the Gentoo Penguin—Pygoscelis Papua).
   b. The moose, (the Alaskan Moose—Alces Gigas).
   c. The Blue Whale.

7. a. A pride of lions.
   b. A drey of squirrels.

8. a. A gaggle of geese.
   b. A covey of partridges.

NATURE LOVERS STOP HERE

9. What is the function of chlorophyll in green plants?

10. Why are fossils found in the amber of the Baltic region of Europe almost perfectly preserved after over 38,000,000 years?

11. What is the name of the process of growth and development whereby a caterpillar becomes a butterfly and a tadpole changes into a frog?

12. Which widespread and rather unpleasant insect became known as 'the steam bug' in Lancashire, the 'Shiner' in Army slang and was called the 'Croton bug' in New York, when it was found to have infested the Croton viaduct, which supplies the city with water?

13. Where in the body would you find?
    a. Your oesophagus.
    b. Your sternum.
    c. Your phagocytes.
    d. Your gluteus maximus.

(4 MARKS)

9. It helps in the process of photosynthesis, possible only in green plants, whereby sugar is produced from carbon dioxide and water, under the influence of light.

10. Insects and spiders, some 38,000,000 years old have been preserved with little or no change in their condition at the time of death. Drops of gummy resin falling from trees trapped the small creatures, and the resin on fossilisation became hard amber.

11. Metamorphosis.

12. The German Cockroach (Blattella Germanica).

13. a. Your oesophagus is the gullet—canal from mouth to stomach.
    b. Your sternum is the breast bone.
    c. Phagocytes are small cells contained in the bloodstream.
    d. The gluteus maximus is the largest muscle in the body—the buttocks!

FOR THOSE WITH AN EAR FOR MUSIC

1. How many keys would you expect to find on the keyboard of a concert grand piano?

2. Which composer had published his first sonatas at the age of seven and had written by the age of twelve, an opera, a symphony and many other shorter works?

3. Name the composer who was court organist at Weimar, and in later life suffered from total blindness before dying of apoplexy.

4. Stravinsky became an American citizen in 1945. From which country did he originate?

5. Which popular conductor has given his name to a West End show based upon his sayings?

6. Name the famous Hungarian composer who took holy orders in 1865.

7. Who wrote the music for the following operas:
   a. *The Barber of Seville*
   b. *The Masked Ball*?

   (2 MARKS)

8. With which type of music do you mainly associate
   a. John Philip Sousa
   b. W. C. Handy?

   (2 MARKS)

FOR THOSE WITH AN EAR FOR MUSIC—ANSWERS

1. 85 (50 white keys and 35 black).

2. Mozart.

3. J. S. Bach.

4. Russia—he was born at Oranienbaum near St Petersburg.

5. *Beecham* by Caryl Brahms and Ned Sherrin, starring Timothy West.

6. Franz Liszt.

7. a. Rossini.
   b. Verdi.

8. a. The march.
   b. The blues.

9. a. The alto saxophone.
   b. The piano.

FOR THOSE WITH AN EAR FOR MUSIC

9. With which musical instrument do you associate these Jazz musicians?
   a. Charlie Parker.
   b. Willie 'The Lion' Smith.

(2 MARKS)

10. Which Jazz musician recorded a memorable version of Rimsky Korsakov's *Flight of the Bumble Bee* on the trumpet?

11. What type of music is referred to as a ' Boston'?

12. With which countries would you associate the following distinctive styles of music?
   a. The Mazurka.
   b. The Fandango.
   c. The Bosa Nova.

(3 MARKS)

13. With which countries would you associate the following national anthems or songs, which are often played at international events?
   a. *Yes we love with fond devotion.*
   b. *The Hope.*
   c. *The Soldier's Song.*

(3 MARKS)

FOR THOSE WITH AN EAR FOR MUSIC—ANSWERS

10. Harry James.

11. A variation of the waltz, known in ballroom dancing as the 'Boston Two Step'.

12. a. Poland.
    b. Spain.
    c. Brazil.

13. a. Norway.
    b. Israel.
    c. Republic of Ireland.

BOOKWORMS BROWSE HERE

1. What is the collective name given to the novels of Sir Walter Scott set in the border country?

2. Who wrote the original words of *Auld Lang Syne*?

3. To which important group of writers did Virginia Woolf, Clive Bell, Roger Fry and Lytton Strachey belong?

4. Name the author whose first major work, *A Textbook of Biology*, was published in 1893. (He later became much better known as one of the earliest Science Fiction writers).

5. With whom did Wordsworth collaborate to write *The Lyrical Ballads*?

6. With which famous poets do you associate the following lines?
   a. 'If Winter comes, can Spring be far behind?'
   b. 'For fools rush in where angels fear to tread.'
   c. 'For men may come and men may go, but I go on for ever.'

   (3 MARKS)

7. Which authors wrote the following modern novels?
   a. *The L-Shaped Room.*
   b. *A Room with a View.*
   c. *Room at the Top.*
   d. *The Small Back Room.*

   (4 MARKS)

BOOKWORMS BROWSE HERE—ANSWERS

1. The 'Waverley' Novels.

2. Robert Burns (1759–96).

3. The Bloomsbury Group.

4. H. G. Wells.

5. S. T. Coleridge.

6. a. Shelley.
   b. Pope.
   c. Lord Tennyson.

7. a. Lynne Reid Banks.
   b. E. M. Forster.
   c. John Braine.
   d. Nigel Balchin.

8. Which famous poet, known equally well as an artist, wrote a poem which was set to music and, despite the title, has become almost a second British national anthem?

9. Name the distinguished Victorian writer who was the son of probably the best-remembered Headmaster of Rugby School.

10. On which actual town did Thomas Hardy base his novel *The Mayor of Casterbridge*?

11. Two of Jane Austen's most celebrated works started life with different titles. Give the well-known names of the books originally called:
a. *Elinor and Marianne*.
b. *First Impressions*.

(2 MARKS)

12. The following literary figures have all been married to one of the others. Rearrange the names in husband and wife combinations:

a. Ted Hughes.	Katherine Mansfield.
b. C. P. Snow.	Sylvia Plath.
c. John Middleton Murry.	Pamela Hansford Johnson.

(3 MARKS)

BOOKWORMS BROWSE HERE—ANSWERS

8. William Blake. The poem was *Jerusalem*.

9. Matthew Arnold.

10. Dorchester.

11. a. *Sense and Sensibility*.
    b. *Pride and Prejudice*.

12. a. Ted Hughes and Sylvia Plath.
    b. C. P. Snow and Pamela Hansford Johnson.
    c. John Middleton Murry and Katherine Mansfield.

FOOD FOR THOUGHT

1. What is the capacity of the human stomach?

2. Which vitamin is commonly known as the 'sunshine' vitamin?

3. What is the stimulant common to tea, coffee and cocoa?

4. Which of the three main nutrients is not present in meat?

5. Which is the most fattening and which the least fattening of the following meals, assuming an equal weight per portion?
   a. Shepherd's Pie. b. Cheese omelette.
   c. Toad-in-the-hole. d. Irish Stew.

   (2 MARKS)

6. Which of the following foods is the best source of Vitamin C and which is the poorest?
   a. New Potatoes. b. Lettuce.
   c. Carrots. d. Apples.

   (2 MARKS)

7. Which of the following drinks contains the most calories and which contains the least?
   a. $^1/_2$ pint beer. b. $^1/_2$ pint milk.
   c. $^1/_2$ pint cider. d. a small tot of whisky.

   (2 MARKS)

8. Select the two most energetic of the following occupations:
   a. Coal-mining. b. Woodcutting.
   c. Walking upstairs. d. Walking briskly.

   (2 MARKS)

FOOD FOR THOUGHT—ANSWERS

1. Approximately 4 pints.

2. Vitamin D: it is produced directly by the action of ultra-violet light on the skin.

3. Caffeine.

4. There are no carbohydrates present in meat.

5. Cheese omelette is the most fattening: 102 calories per ounce.
   Shepherd's Pie is the least fattening: 32 calories per ounce.
   Toad-in-the-hole: 86 calories per ounce.
   Irish Stew: 42 calories per ounce.

6. New potatoes are the best source of vitamin C: 9 mgms per ounce.
   Apples are the poorest: 1 mgm per ounce.
   Lettuce: 4 mgms per ounce.
   Carrots: 3 mgms per ounce.

7. A half pint of milk contains the most calories: 180.
   A small tot of whisky contains the least: 75.
   1/2 pint beer: 150 calories.
   1/2 pint cider: 120 calories.

8. Walking upstairs is the most energetic of these occupations, followed by woodcutting.
   Walking upstairs: 1,000 calories per hour.
   Woodcutting: 380 calories per hour.
   Coal-mining: 320 calories per hour.
   Walking briskly: 215 calories per hour.

9. Iron, calcium, iodine and thiamin (Vitamin B1) are all essential to the diet. Their absence can lead to serious deficiency diseases. Which of the following diseases is caused by the deficiency of which substance?
   a. Goitre.
   b. Beri-Beri.
   c. Rickets.
   d. Anaemia.

(4 MARKS)

10. The following statements are all true, but can you explain why?
    a. Raw food may be of greater nutritional value than the same type of food served cooked.
    b. The average man requires more food than the average woman.
    c. If more protein is eaten than is needed for an individual's immediate requirements, some of it will be converted to body fat.
    d. It is possible to tell that one cabbage contains more Vitamin A than another simply by looking at it.

(4 MARKS)

FOOD FOR THOUGHT—ANSWERS

9. a. Iodine.
   b. Thiamin.
   c. Calcium.
   d. Iron.

10. a. Heat destroys many constituents of food, particularly some vitamins.
    b. The energy requirement of different people is proportional to the surface area of the individual body. As men are in general bigger than women, the total number of calories required by the average man is greater than the total needed by the average woman.
    c. All the major nutrients, (fats, carbohydrates and proteins), can only be stored in the form of fat by the body.
    d. In green vegetables, the amount of Vitamin A is proportional to their greenness.

VINTAGE STUFF FOR WINE BUFFS

1. Which of the European wine-growing countries produces the greatest quantity of wine?

2. In which province of Spain is sherry produced?

3. Why are the green wines of Portugal thus called?

4. Are there legal restrictions regarding the pasteurisation of wine?

5. Two of the following were top vintage years for claret. Identify the vintage years from the following.
   a. 1945 b. 1954
   c. 1960 d. 1961

   (2 MARKS)

6. What are the three classes of wine as defined in the Code de Vin which forms an integral part of French law?

   (3 MARKS)

7. What serving temperatures are recommended by the leading authorities (Larousse Gastronomique) for the following wines?
   a. Vintage claret.
   b. Champagne.
   c. Sweet white wine.

   (3 MARKS)

VINTAGE STUFF FOR WINE BUFFS—ANSWERS

1. Italy.

2. Cadiz. (Principally in Jerez, which is an area in this province).

3. The name does not refer to the colour but rather to the lightness and acidulous freshness of the wine; it should be drunk young and cool.

4. No. Pasteurisation of wine is normally carried out, usually between 55 and 70 degrees Centigrade, but this is not a legal requirement.

5. 1945 and 1961.

6.

Vins de pays (du canton de)	Locally grown
Vins de coupage	Blended wines
Vins d'appellation d'origine	Superior wines. Exclusive title to Geographical name.

7.

a. Vintage claret	16–18 C (61–64.5 F)
b. Champagne	5–7 C (41–45 F)
c. Sweet white wine	2–5 C (36–41 F)

8. Why are bottles of wine properly stored lying on their sides?

9. What exactly is Slivovic, the national drink of Yugoslavia?

10. How many degrees proof are the well-known proprietary brands of whisky and gin sold in this country?

11. When Prince Charlie came to Scotland in 1745, he presented the recipe of his personal liqueur to a MacKinnon of Skye as a reward for services rendered to the Prince. This recipe has been kept within the MacKinnon family and the liqueur is still manufactured today. What is the name of this traditional Scottish drink?

12. What is the principal ingredient in a 'Manhattan' cocktail?

13. Crème de Menthe is noted for its strong characteristic flavour of peppermint. There are other liqueurs with distinctive flavours such as blackcurrant, aniseed, orange, herbs, plums and coffee. With which flavour would you associate the following liqueurs?
    a. Tia Maria.
    b. Cointreau.
    c. Crème de Cassis.

(3 MARKS)

8. To keep the wine in contact with the cork, thus preventing it from drying out.

9. Plum Brandy.

10. 70°.

11. Drambuie, (translated into Gaelic 'the drink that satisfies').

12. Whisky. (Scotch, Rye or Bourbon).

13. a. Coffee.
    b. Orange.
    c. Blackcurrant.

TRAVEL BROADENS THE MIND

1. What percentage of the world's surface is covered by water? Is it 34%, 57%, or 71%?

2. In which country are some of the residents known as Walloons?

3. What is the name of the other airport, besides Kennedy, which serves New York City?

4. Which country would you visit to explore the deserted Inca city of Machu Picchu?

5. Tehran is the capital of Iran; of which country is Tirane the capital city?

6. To which country would you travel if you wished to see the wild life in the Meru National Park and Samburu?

7. In which Italian cities are the following tourist attractions:
   a. The Bridge of Sighs
   b. The Spanish Steps
   c. The Piazza Della Signoria?

   (3 MARKS)

8. Besides Lithuania and Latvia, which was the other neighbouring Baltic State which was incorporated into the USSR after the last war?

9. Which country would you visit to enjoy the ancient cities of Marrakesh and Agadir?

10. Which country is made up of the three main islands of Kyushu, Kyoto and Hokkaido?

TRAVEL BROADENS THE MIND—ANSWERS

1. 71%.
2. Belgium.
3. La Guardia Airport.
4. Peru. Machu Picchu means literally, 'the lost city of the Incas'.
5. Tirane, (or Tirana) is the Capital of Albania.
6. Kenya.
7. a. Venice.
   b. Rome.
   c. Florence.
8. Estonia.
9. Morocco.
10. Japan.

11. Into what national currency would you need to change your money if you were travelling in the following countries?
    a. Argentina.
    b. Holland.
    c. United Arab Emirates.

    (3 MARKS)

12. Which country is famous for its polders?

13. Which area of the United States is closest to the USSR?—geographically, of course!

14. Where would you go to visit Victoria Land or Queen Maud Land?

15. In the area of which country—outside the British Isles—would you find in close proximity: Liverpool, Windsor, Penrith, Lithow and Swansea?

16. Where would you have to travel if you wished to observe the Sea of Tranquillity?

TRAVEL BROADENS THE MIND—ANSWERS

11. a. Peso.
    b. Guilder.
    c. Dirham.

12. Holland. A polder is an area of land reclaimed from the sea and protected by dykes.

13. Alaska. It is only separated from Russia's Eastern Border by the Bering Sea.

14. Antarctica.

15. New South Wales, Australia.

16. Space: it is on the Moon.

FOR THE CULTURE VULTURE

1. Who is generally regarded as the founder of the Post-impressionist school of painters?

2. Name the sculptor whose major works include: *The Thinker*, *The Kiss*, and *The Hand of God*.

3. Name the French Impressionist painter who painted well-known pictures of Waterloo and the Houses of Parliament.

4. Which artist painted the controversial portrait of Sir Winston Churchill, which was later deliberately destroyed by Lady Churchill?

5. Name the English landscape artist who lived and was buried in Hampstead and painted many famous pictures of Hampstead Heath.

6. Which famous English sculptor and painter was the official war artist between 1940 and 1942, and produced a series of drawings of shelterers in the London Tube stations?

7. In which city would you find the following Art Galleries?
   a. Whitney.
   b. Uffizi.

   (2 MARKS)

8. In which famous Art Galleries would you be able to see
   a. The *Mona Lisa* Leonardo da Vinci
   b. *Fishing boats endeavouring to rescue the crew* J. M. W. Turner
   c. *Charles I* Van Dyck
   d. *St Peter and St Paul* El Greco?

   (4 MARKS)

FOR THE CULTURE VULTURE—ANSWERS

1. Paul Cezanne (1839–1906).

2. A. Rodin (1840–1917).

3. Claude Monet.

4. Graham Sutherland.

5. John Constable.

6. Henry Moore.

7. a. New York.
   b. Florence.

8. a. The Louvre in Paris.
   b. The Tate Gallery in London.
   c. The National Gallery in London.
   d. The Hermitage Gallery in Leningrad.

9. Identify the famous English painters from the following information:
   a. Who lived in a Berkshire village, carried his equipment around in a pram, and claimed that his inspiration came to him through religious joy?
   b. Who depicted in his work both 'the Harlot's Progress' and 'the Rake's Progress'?
   c. Who had a reputation as one of this country's finest portrait artists, whose subjects included Dr Johnson, Laurence Sterne and Edmund Burke?

(3 MARKS)

10. Identify the famous artists and sculptors from the Renaissance period, who are responsible for the following works of art, all to be seen in Florence:
    a. *David* the Marble statue in the Academy.
    b. *David* the Bronze nude statue with the head of Goliath in the National Museum.
    c. *The Urbino Venus* the painting in the Uffizi Gallery.

(3 MARKS)

11. Who depicted in his work: six apparitions of Lenin on a piano; a portrait of Gala with two lamb chops on her shoulder and a lobster telephone?

12. Corot, Rousseau and Millet were all associated with a particular school of painting named after a village near Paris, in which all three artists lived. What is it called?

9. a. Stanley Spencer.
   b. William Hogarth.
   c. Joshua Reynolds.

10. a. Michelangelo.
    b. Donatello.
    c. Titian.

11. Salvador Dali.

12. Barbizon.

THE SCIENTIFIC WAY

1. At what temperature do the Centigrade and Fahrenheit scales register an identical reading?

2. Which of the following scientists do you associate with the principles of static electricity: Joseph Priestley, Henry Cavendish, Lord Kelvin or Archimedes?

3. Who is popularly known as the 'father of chemistry'?

4. Chalk, marble and limestone are the natural forms of which chemical?

5. Diamonds and charcoal are different forms of one of the elements. Which element is this?

6. Which scientist adapted the principles of heat radiation in order to invent the first thermos flask?

7. Which chemicals form the major part of the following familiar household products?
   a. Vinegar.
   b. Washing soda.
   c. Baking powder.

   (3 MARKS)

8. For what scientific purpose would you use the following?
   a. An anemometer.
   b. An hydrometer.
   c. A galvanometer.

   (3 MARKS)

THE SCIENTIFIC WAY—ANSWERS

1. Minus 40 degrees.
2. Lord Kelvin.
3. Robert Boyle 1627–1691.
4. Calcium carbonate.
5. Carbon.
6. Sir James Dewar.
7. a. Acetic acid.
   b. Sodium carbonate.
   c. Sodium bicarbonate.
8. a. To measure wind speed.
   b. To measure the specific gravity of a liquid.
   c. To detect and measure an electric current.

9. With which prominent scientists would you associate these important scientific laws?
   a. The three laws of motion.
   b. The upthrust of an object immersed in a liquid is equal to the weight of liquid which it displaces.
   c. The laws of gases—relating pressure and volume.
   d. The law of the theory of electrical current and the resistance of a conductor of electricity.

(4 MARKS)

10. The remaining space in this Section is devoted to 'Outer Space':
    a. Do the planets and asteroids in our solar system revolve around the sun in a clockwise or anticlockwise direction?
    b. Which is the largest planet in our solar system?
    c. Which planet is nearest to earth?
    d. Which planet, apart from earth, do scientists consider may have conditions which could sustain life?

(4 MARKS)

9. a. Sir Isaac Newton, 1642–1727.
   b. Archimedes, 287–212 BC.
   c. Robert Boyle, 1627–1691.
   d. Georg Simon Ohm, 1787–1854.

10. a. Anticlockwise (looking on the eliptic from North).
    b. Jupiter.
    c. Venus.
    d. Mars.

FUN SECTION

SPOT THE STAR	(Identify a personality from clues)
WHO SAID?	(Quotations)
WHAT'S THE LINK?	(Find the connection between a number of personalities or objects)
WHEN OR WHERE?	(Famous occasions)
LUCKY DIP	(Select a correct answer from the alternatives)
ODD MAN OUT	(Pick the outsider from a group)
MOTORWAY MADNESS	(Illustrations)
YOU'LL KICK YOURSELF	(Trick questions)

SPOT THE STAR

1. Who was born into a poor family in Tupelo in 1935, won second prize in a talent contest at the age of ten, and two years later was given his first guitar because his parents could not afford the bike which he had asked for?

2. Which actress was chosen to play the part of Desdemona at the National Theatre, opposite Paul Scofield, after playing at playing the part in James Ivory's film *Shakespeare Wallah*?

3. Who was born in Limerick, the son of a grocery store manager, became a well-known compere and TV quizmaster and made a hit record with a song previously recorded by the Brighouse and Rastrick Brass Band?

4. Who was born in Paris, the youngest of nine children of a house painter, broke into show business as an acrobat but later became established as a singer and comedian in films?

5. Who appeared on stage in a musical about a mental patient, played in goal for his school football team and was sent off every week for what is now called 'dissent' and drove a Rolls Royce into a swimming pool in his television comedy series?

6. Who used to be a football correspondent for the *Observer*, ran a successful night club, is acknowledged as an expert on food and has a very strong link with the Isle of Ely?

7. Who was noted for his ability to consume 27 pork chops and a bottle of gin at one sitting, had ten brothers and sisters and was the subject of a musical show in celebration of his life and times which played recently in the West End?

SPOT THE STAR—ANSWERS

1. Elvis Presley.
2. Felicity Kendal.
3. Terry Wogan.
4. Maurice Chevalier.
5. Michael Crawford.
6. Clement Freud.
7. Fats Waller.

8. Who was the actor, born in Alexandria with the real name of Michael Shalhoub, who developed a weakness for gambling and bought his own casino, and is also an expert at the game of bridge?

9. Who was born the daughter of a New York policeman, was spotted in the chorus line of Broadway's *George White's Scandals* by Rudy Vallee and appeared in a string of lively film musicals, notably *Alexander's Ragtime Band*, the archetypal chronicle musical with 26 great songs?

10. Who was the most popular cartoon character of the screen before the reign of Mickey Mouse, was first introduced in 1914 by animator Pat Sullivan and recently made a comeback on American Television?

11. Who is host each week to a variety of international musicians, has established a reputation as author, wit and raconteur, speaks disparagingly about the food served in his own Club—'even the mice eat next door!'—and remains one of this country's leading exponents of the tenor saxophone?

12. Who is fond of wearing a pink bow tie, was one half of a most successful radio comedy script-writing team, and is now a long-standing regular on several popular panel games?

13. Who won her first beauty contest at the age of 14, started in Hollywood in 1963 by landing small parts in two films, appointed and then married a brilliant press agent who has helped her to become a star and a leading sex symbol?

8. Omar Sharif.

9. Alice Faye.

10. Felix the Cat.

11. Ronnie Scott.

12. Frank Muir.

13. Raquel Welch.

14. Who was the second son of a wealthy inventor and beautiful concert pianist, made his Broadway debut in 1934 as Tybalt in *Romeo and Juliet*, while still a young man starred in and directed a film which is widely regarded as a classic of the cinema, and played the part of the enigmatic Harry Lime in Carol Reed's film *The Third Man* made in 1949?

15. Who was the intelligent and good-looking male recruited from among 300 candidates to play the heroine of the 1943 screen adaptation of an Eric Knight novel—the success of the film being such that there have been six sequels and the part has been played by four of his descendants? (He was described by one reviewer as 'Greer Garson in Fur', has never spoken a word, but his bark is much better than his bite.)

16. Who is an actor, director, screen writer, playwright and jazz clarinetist, wrote jokes for newspaper columnists and contributed sketches for revues before performing his own material in Greenwich Village cafés in his native New York? (He received the best picture Oscar and major commercial success for a film released in 1977 but many critics consider a later film, depicting his home city, to be the finest he has made.)

17. Identify the authors from the titles of the following autobiographies.
    a. *Bring on the Empty Horses*
    b. *Day by Day.*
    c. *Farce from my Elbow.*
    d. *With a Little Bit of Luck.*

(4 MARKS)

SPOT THE STAR—ANSWERS

14. Orson Welles.

15. Lassie (Real name Pal).

16. Woody Allen.

17. a. David Niven.
    b. Robin Day.
    c. Brian Rix.
    d. Stanley Holloway.

WHO SAID?

1. Who described patriotism as 'the last refuge of a scoundrel'?

2. Which famous playwright, raconteur and wit reflected: 'When people agree with me I always feel that I must be wrong'?

3. Who said of Richard Milhous Nixon: 'A truly impressive brain and certainly a far better President of the United States than John F. Kennedy'?
   a. Lord Longford. b. Henry Kissinger.
   c. Alistair Cooke. d. Anthony Howard.

4. Who said 'A psychiatrist is a man who goes to the Folies Bergere and looks at the audience?'
   a. Jack Benny. b. George Bernard Shaw.
   c. Mervyn Stockwood. d. Maurice Chevalier.

5. The following statements were made by four prominent politicians: Harold Wilson, Tony Benn, Sir Geoffrey Howe and Sir Winston Churchill. Who said what?
   a. 'God knows, Government can't do it all.'
   b. 'Britain today is suffering from galloping obsolescence.'
   c. 'Perhaps it is better to be irresponsible and right than to be responsible and wrong.'
   d. 'Everybody should have an equal chance but they shouldn't have a flying start.'

(4 MARKS)

6. The following remarks are attributed to four famous comedians: Groucho Marx, Spike Milligan, Marty Feldman and W. C. Fields. Which comic made which comment?
   a. 'Anybody who hates children and dogs can't be all bad.'

WHO SAID?—ANSWERS

1. Samuel Johnson.

2. Oscar Wilde.

3. Lord Longford (Atticus interview, *Sunday Times*, 13th April 1980.)

4. Mervyn Stockwood, 1961.

5. a. Sir Geoffrey Howe on spending cuts, *Observer*, 4th June 1979.
   b. Tony Benn, 2nd February 1963.
   c. Winston Churchill in a radio broadcast, 26th August 1950.
   d. Harold Wilson, 1963.

b. 'Comedy, like sodomy, is an unnatural act.'
c. 'Please accept my resignation. I don't want to belong to any club that will accept me as a member.'
d. 'I shook hands with a friendly Arab ... I still have my right hand to prove it.'

(4 MARKS)

7. The following quotations were given by The Duke of Edinburgh, King George V, King Edward VII and King Edward VIII. Which remark was made by which Royal personage?
a. 'If I had to live in conditions like that I would be a revolutionary myself.'
b. 'There is no central machinery to promote a substitute for a good neighbour.'
c. 'I never see any home cooking. All I get is the fancy stuff.'
d. 'You can tell when you have crossed the frontier into Germany because of the badness of the coffee.'

(4 MARKS)

8. The following remarks about children were written by Bernard Shaw, Ogden Nash, Jean-Paul Sartre and Oscar Wilde. Which writer wrote which piece?
a. 'I must have been an insufferable child; all children are.'
b. 'All children know they are progressing. Moreover, they're not allowed to forget it.'
c. 'Parents were invented to make children happy by giving them something to ignore.'
d. 'Children begin by loving their parents. After a time they judge them. Rarely, if ever, do they forgive them.'

(4 MARKS)

WHO SAID?—ANSWERS

6. a. W. C. Fields in the *Radio Times*, 12th August 1965.
   b. Marty Feldman, 9th June 1969.
   c. Groucho Marx, (in a telegram).
   d. Spike Milligan.

7. a. George V, (quoted by L. MacNeil Weir).
   b. Edward VIII, (*Observer*, May 1953).
   c. Duke of Edinburgh, (*Observer*, December 1962).
   d. Edward VII, (quoted by Lord Holdane).

8. a. Bernard Shaw.
   b. Jean-Paul Sartre.
   c. Ogden Nash.
   d. Oscar Wilde.

WHAT'S THE LINK?

1. What do the following personalities have in common?
   a. Sir Alec Douglas-Home.
   b. James Goldsmith.
   c. Humphrey Lyttelton.
   d. David Benedictus.

2. What do these well-known bridges have in common?
   a. The Bridge of San Luis Rey.
   b. Waterloo Bridge.
   c. The Bridge on the River Kwai.

3. What do the Mistral, the Haboob and the Sirocco have in common?

4. Great Britain competes for the following trophies in international sporting events. What do they have in common?
   a. The Curtis Cup (Golf).
   b. The Wightman Cup (Tennis).
   c. The Uber Cup (Badminton).

5. Don Revie and Brian Clough were both managers of the same club at one stage of their careers. They also both played for another well-known Northern team, before they became managers. Name the two football teams which link these two personalities.

   (2 MARKS)

6. John Wilkes Booth and Lee Harvey Oswald are linked in several ways:
   a. For what crimes are they both remembered?
   b. Were they both raised in the North or South of the USA?
   c. How did they both die?

   (3 MARKS)

WHAT'S THE LINK?—ANSWERS

1. All are old Etonians.

2. All are the titles of films.

3. All are the names of winds.

4. All are ladies' events.

5. Leeds United and Sunderland.

6. a. Both shot American Presidents in the head. Booth killed President Lincoln and Oswald killed President Kennedy.
   b. Both were Southerners. Booth born 1839 and Oswald in 1939.
   c. Both were murdered before being brought to trial.

7. The following well-known personalities, from different walks of life, share the same Christian name and surname. Can you identify?
   a. An ex-England test cricketer; and top political leader?
   b. A trade union official, now retired; and a popular singer?
   c. A musician; and a politician who also happens to be a musician?
   d. An Australian test cricketer; and an ex-international English footballer?

(4 MARKS)

8. What would you be buying if you purchased some: Rough Fell, Lonk, Derbyshire Gritstone, or Kerry Hill?

9. What do *Years of Victory*, *The Years of Endurance* and *The Age of Elegance* have in common?

10. What do the terms 'litotes', 'hyperbole', 'alliteration', 'personification' and 'onomatopoeia' describe?

11. What would you be doing if performing any of the following: A Halling, A Landler, A Strathspey?

12. Who would you expect to be able to produce the following: A Sheet Bend, A Timber Hitch, A Square Trestle?

13. With what do you associate the following: Bloodnok, Minnie, Bluebottle and Crun?

14. With what activity do you associate the following: Bantam, Fly, Feather?

7. a. David Steele.
   b. Jack Jones.
   c. Ted Heath.
   d. Rodney Marsh.

8. All are breeds of British Sheep.

9. All refer to periods of British History described in his books by Arthur Bryant.

10. All are figures of speech or stylistic devices which may be employed by a writer.

11. All are dances derived from different countries.

12. A Scout. All are knots, hitches etc used in pioneering.

13. All are characters from *The Goon Show*.

14. All are weight categories used in the sport of boxing.

WHEN OR WHERE?

1. In what year did the Sex Discrimination Act come into force?

2. Where would you expect a kilted Scotsman to keep his money?

3. In what year were the first female traffic wardens introduced into this country?

4. Where would you find the largest castle in England?

5. In what year was the last débutante presented at Court?

6. Where would you literally find Hell on Earth?

7. Where would you be most likely to find:
   a. Hula-hula girls.
   b. Mancunians.
   c. A Sonteneur?

(3 MARKS)

WHEN OR WHERE?—ANSWERS

1. 1975, 29th December.

2. In his sporran.

3. 1964. Male traffic wardens first appeared in 1960.

4. Windsor.

5. 1958.

6. It is a small hamlet near Trondheim, in Norway.

7. a. Hawaii (dancing girls
   b. Manchester.
   c. A red light area: a sonteneur is a pimp.

8. In which country would you be most likely to find:
   a. A Stakhanovite.
   b. A Khidmutgar.
   c. A Kauri.
   d. A Meerkat.

(4 MARKS)

9. In which year did the following events take place?
   a. Stephenson's Rocket made its first journey:
      1819, 1829 or 1851?
   b. Women over 30 first obtained the vote:
      1918, 1923 or 1925?
   c. Eton College was founded:
      1440, 1620 or 1834?
   d. Christopher Columbus discovered the New World:
      1385, 1492 or 1523?

(4 MARKS)

10. We ask you now to suggest a famous occasion when it is possible the following remarks—which we have invented—could have been made?
   a. 'That's the last time I let that man in my kitchen.'
   b. 'We seem to have two of everything except the fish.'
   c. 'Don't worry, Ma'am. It was due to go to the cleaners anyway.'

(5 MARKS)

8. a. Russia. A Stakhanovite is a Russian worker who increases his output by a considerable extent.
   b. India. A Khidmutgar is a male table servant in India.
   c. New Zealand. A Kauri is a coniferous timber tree indigenous to New Zealand.
   d. South Africa. A Meerkat is a small mammal found mainly in South Africa.

9. a. 1829.
   b. 1918.
   c. 1440.
   d. 1492.

10. a. On the occasion when King Alfred burnt the cakes.
    b. On the occasion when Noah took all the animals into the Ark.
    c. On the occasion when Sir Walter Raleigh laid his cloak over a puddle for Queen Elizabeth I.

LUCKY DIP

1. Beatrice Webb was?
   a. Winston Churchill's nanny.
   b. A distinguished social reformer.
   c. An actress with the Royal Shakespeare Company.

2. Charles Blondin was?
   a. A notorious criminal at the turn of the century.
   b. A silent film star who appeared in movies with Chaplin.
   c. The first man to cross the Niagra Falls on a tightrope.

3. John Speke was?
   a. The man who discovered the source of the Nile.
   b. The surgeon who removed a gall stone from Queen Victoria.
   c. A famous art collector.

4. Ellen Cicely Wilkinson was?
   a. A titled young lady spoken of as a likely match for Prince Charles.
   b. Minister of Education in the Attlee Cabinet.
   c. An executive with a major cosmetics firm.

5. Michael Augustine Corrigan was?
   a. The third Roman Catholic Archbishop of New York.
   b. The first person to take out a patent for the string vest.
   c. The founder of the temperance movement.

6. Vicompte Ferdinand de Lesseps was?
   a. The engineer who designed the Suez Canal.
   b. The first victim of the French Revolution.
   c. Captain of the victorious 1963 French Rugby team.

7. What is the length of Hadrian's Wall?
   a. 98 miles. b. 123 miles.
   c. $73^1/_2$ miles. d. 108 miles.

LUCKY DIP—ANSWERS

1. A distinguished social reformer.

2. The first man to cross the Niagara Falls on a tightrope.

3. The man who discovered the source of the Nile.

4. Minister of Education in the Attlee Cabinet.

5. The third Roman Catholic Archbishop of New York.

6. The engineer who designed the Suez Canal.

7. $73\frac{1}{2}$ miles.

8. What is the length of the Grand Canyon in America?
   a. 217 miles. b. 312 miles.
   c. 429 miles. d. 530 miles.

9. How many feet does the Leaning Tower of Pisa deviate from the perpendicular?
   a. 20. b. 16. c. 12.

10. How high is the cross on the dome of St Paul's Cathedral?
    a. 363 feet. b. 482 feet. c. 590 feet.

11. How high is the platform at the summit of the Eiffel Tower?
    a. 748 feet. b. 985 feet. c. 1,023 feet.

12. How high is Mount Everest?
    a. 29,028 feet. b. 33,553 feet. c. 36,071 feet.

13. Rearrange the following so that the inventor corresponds to the *appropriate* invention:

a. Sir Richard Arkwright	Antiseptic Surgery.
b. James Outram	The telephone.
c. Sir Joseph Lister	Cotton-Spinning Machine.
d. Alexander Graham Bell	Tramways.

(4 MARKS)

14. Re-arrange the following descriptions to correspond with the *appropriate* object:

a. Scimitar	A large rat.
b. Asymptote	A small coin.
c. Bandicoot	A short curved oriental sword.
d. Picayune	A line that approaches but does not meet a given curve.

(4 MARKS)

8. 217 miles.

9. 16.

10. 363 feet.

11. 985 feet.

12. 29,028 feet.

13. a. Sir Richard Arkwright invented the Cotton-Spinning Machine.
    b. James Outram invented tramways.
    c. Sir Joseph Lister first used antiseptic surgery.
    d. Alexander Graham Bell invented the telephone.

14. a. A scimitar is a short curved oriental sword.
    b. Asymptote is the name of a line that approaches but does not meet a given curve.
    c. A bandicoot is a large rat.
    d. A picayune is a small coin.

ODD MAN OUT

1. Which of the following politicians is the odd man out?
   a. Winston Churchill. b. Enoch Powell.
   c. Reg Prentice. d. Jo Grimond.

2. Which of the following ladies is the odd one out?
   a. Catherine of Aragon. b. Anne Boleyn.
   c. Mary Queen of Scots. d. Lady Jane Grey.

3. Which island should not be included in this list?
   a. Manhattan. b. Long Island.
   c. Canvey Island. d. Brooklyn.

4. Which of the following hit records failed to reach Number 1 in the British charts?
   a. *Where are you now (My Love)?* Jackie Trent
   b. *Summer Nights* John Travolta & Olivia Newton-John
   c. *Silence is Golden* Tremeloes
   d. *Please Please Me* The Beatles

5. All of the following villages actually exist in the British Isles, with one exception. Which is the odd man out?
   a. Upper Wriggle Brook (Herefordshire)
   b. Adel Cum Eccup (Near Leeds)
   c. Muddle-on-the-Marsh (Worcestershire)
   d. Fanybedwell (Near Denbigh)
   e. Muck (Galway)
   f. Auld Wives Lift (Stirlingshire)

6. Which of the following invertebrates is the odd man out?
   a. Lobster. b. Starfish.
   c. Centipede. d. Scorpion.

ODD MAN OUT—ANSWERS

1. Jo Grimond is the only one not to have represented the Conservative party in the House of Commons. All the others have represented more than one party.

2. Catherine of Aragon was the only one of these ladies not to be beheaded.

3. Canvey Island is in the Thames Estuary. All the others are part of New York.

4. The highest position achieved by *Please Please Me* by The Beatles was number two.

5. Muddle-on-the-Marsh does not exist.

6. The Starfish is of the phylum ECHINODERMATA (Spiny-skinned). All the others are ARTHROPODS (jointed limbs, segmented body).

7. Which of the following jazz luminaries is the odd man out?
   a. Thad Jones. b. Max Jones.
   c. Elvin Jones. d. Hank Jones.

8. Which tune title is by a different composer from the others?
   a. *Blue Moon.* b. *Where or When.*
   c. *Get Out of Town.* d. *Sing for your Supper.*

9. Which of these novels is the odd man out?
   a. *Sense and Sensibility.* b. *Clarissa.*
   c. *Emma.* d. *Northanger Abbey.*

10. Which of these sportsmen is the odd man out?
    a. Ray Reardon. b. Graham Miles.
    c. Terry Griffiths. d. Jack Charlton.

11. Which of these plays is the odd man out?
    a. *Lady Windermere's Fan.* b. *Widowers' Houses.*
    c. *Mrs Warren's Profession.* d. *Doctor's Dilemma.*

12. Which of the following films is the odd man out?
    a. *The African Queen.* b. *Casablanca.*
    c. *Adam's Rib.* d. *High Sierra.*

ODD MAN OUT—ANSWERS

7. Max Jones is a British jazz critic; all the others are brothers and American jazz musicians.

8. *Get Out of Town* was written by Cole Porter. All the others are by Richard Rodgers.

9. *Clarissa* was written by Samuel Richardson. All the others are novels by Jane Austen.

10. Jack Charlton is a footballer (Eddie Charlton plays snooker). All the others are top professional snooker players.

11. *Lady Windermere's Fan* is by Oscar Wilde. All the others are by G. B. Shaw.

12. *Adam's Rib* is the only film not to star Humphrey Bogart.

13. Which of the following names is the Odd Man Out?
 a. Sir Peter Teazle. b. Crabtree.
 c. Sir Benjamin Backbite. d. Puff.

14. Which of the following Colleges is NOT in Cambridge?
 a. St Johns. b. Emmanuel.
 c. Selwyn. d. Lincoln.

15. Which of the following does NOT appear in Chaucer's *Prologue* & *Canterbury Tales*?
 a. The Minstrel. b. The Pardoner.
 c. The Friar. d. The Reeve.

16. Which of these musicians is not a distinguished guitarist?
 a. John Williams. b. Stephane Grappelli.
 c. Joe Pass. d. Segovia.

17. Which of these places of entertainment in London is the odd man out?
 a. The Globe. b. The Empire.
 c. The Duchess. d. The Haymarket.

18. Which of the following is not the name of a station on the London Underground system?
 a. Snaresbrook. b. Parsons Green.
 c. Roosters End. d. Stonebridge Park.

19. Which of the following is not the name of an International Airline?
 a. Qantas. b. Iberia.
 c. Lufthansa. d. Salina.

20. Which of the following famous buildings is not used as a place of worship?
 a. City Temple. b. York Minster.
 c. Kingsway Hall. d. Benthall Hall.

13. Puff is a character from Sheridan's *The Critic*. All the others appear in *The School for Scandal*.

14. Lincoln is a College in Oxford.

15. The Minstrel.

16. Stephane Grappelli is a violinist.

17. The Empire is a cinema, the others are theatres.

18. Roosters End.

19. Salina.

20. Benthall Hall is a National Trust property in Shropshire.

MOTORWAY MADNESS

Substitute the correct meaning of these road signs.

1 
Don't fall asleep at the wheel!

2 
Beware Red Indians!

3 
Watch out he's digging your grave!

4 
Balloonists dropping

5 
Beware Flying motorbikes

6 
It's quicker by rail

7 
Cyclists only

8 
Living bra!

9 

10-1 you don't make it!

10 
Tea up!

11 
Coach parties welcome

12 
Red Cross station

13 
More Red Indians!

14 
Get out and walk!

15 
Get off and milk it!

16 
Struck by lightning!

17 

Comfort station!

18 

No police patrols

19 
Look what happened to him!

20 
The Lone Ranger rides again!

MOTORWAY MADNESS—ANSWERS

1. Series of bends.
2. Two-way traffic straight ahead.
3. Road works.
4. Danger.
5. All motor vehicles prohibited.
6. Level crossing without gate or barrier ahead.
7. No cycling or moped riding.
8. Uneven road.
9. Steep hill downwards.
10. T Junction.
11. Buses and coaches prohibited.
12. Crossroads.
13. Pass either side.
14. Pedestrian crossing.
15. Cattle.
16. Overhead electric cable.
17. Parking place.
18. Road clear.
19. Quayside or river bank.
20. Horses or ponies.

YOU'LL KICK YOURSELF

1. What is the colour of a peacock's egg?

2. If it takes six men four hours to dig a hole, how long will it take four men to dig half a hole?

3. How many pork pies could a starving man eat on an empty stomach?

4. O. T. T. F. F.—
What is the next letter in this sequence?

5. Which object can be described as having no beginning and no end?

6. If it takes 3 cats 3 minutes to catch 3 mice, how long will it take 10 cats to catch 10 mice?

7. A rancher had five hundred head of cattle and all but thirty three died. How many did he have left?

8. Which is the longest measurement: a rod, pole or perch?

9. If a tortoise and a hare were to compete against the clock over a distance of 100 metres, which animal would have the furthest to go?

10. How much soil would there be in a ditch 100 metres long, 10 metres wide and 5 metres deep?

11. Which weighs most: a ton of feathers or a ton of bricks?

12. Two workers from the same factory live in the same village. One factory worker is the father of the other factory worker's son. How are they related?

YOU'LL KICK YOURSELF—ANSWERS

1. The peacock is the male of the species and does not lay eggs.

2. There is no such thing as half a hole.

3. One. After eating one pie his stomach would no longer be empty.

4. The letters are the initials of the first five numbers, so the next in sequence is S for six.

5. A circle.

6. 3 minutes.

7. 33.

8. All the same.

9. Both would travel 100 metres.

10. There is no soil in the empty ditch.

11. Both weigh one ton.

12. Husband and wife.

13. How many articles would you receive if you were given the old fashioned 'Baker's Dozen'?

14. What kind of music would you expect to hear played by a Junior Jazz Band?

15. If a merchant exchanged 4 pecks of corn for a bushel, would he make a profit or a loss?

16. What has two wings and twenty-two legs?

17. Which would you rather give away, a florin or a crown?

18. If the top temperature today is 70° F and tomorrow's weather forecast promises a maximum of 20° C, which day would you expect to be the warmer?

19. If a watch loses two minutes every hour, stops at half past twelve in the afternoon while it is running half an hour slow, at what time would the watch next show the correct time, if no attempt were made to rewind it?

20. Finally, a traditional riddle, but are you sure that you know the answer? What is black and white and red all over?

13. Thirteen. In the old days the baker would give an extra roll or scone, free of charge, if a dozen were ordered.

14. Junior Jazz Bands are the children's marching bands which flourished in the thirties. They were revived in the fifties and are strong in mining areas of the east midlands and the north-east. The groups are called jazz bands not because they play jazz but because they wear jazzy uniforms. They play music to accompany their marching, using the kazoo (which makes a noise like comb and paper), a type of glockenspiel, drums and cymbals.

15. Neither. A bushel represents 8 gallons (dry measurement) while a peck is 2 gallons. 4 pecks are therefore equal to a bushel.

16. A football team.

17. A florin (two shillings or 10p). (A crown is equal to five shillings or 25p).
Philanthropists should award themselves a bonus mark for giving the wrong answer.

18. Today should be warmer. 20° C is equivalent to 68° F. The weather forecast has, however, been known to be wrong!

19. Midnight.

20. Could it be a sunburnt zebra? A newspaper is black and white and *READ* all over!